IDIOMANIA

by Matthew Harris

MindSync
An Imprint of Oprelle Publications (USA) LLC
236 Twin Hills Road
Grindstone, PA 15442

The content within this publication is solely the work of the author, who is responsible for the accuracy and interpretation of all text, including any examples of idioms or phrases. With intention, several nonsense words were used on the cover to capture reader's attention.

Additionally, all artwork featured on the cover and throughout the interior of this publication was generated using ChatGPT's DALL·E tool and Clipdrop by Jasper. Oprelle Publishing disclaims any liability for the artistic representations and encourages readers to interpret them within the context of the author's narrative.

FIRST EDITION

Printed in the United States of America
ISBN: 979-8-9899015-7-9

This book is dedicated to the memory of Donald Franklin Fisher, my papaw.

He was, and always will be, "the man."

Or what about a ham in a jam?

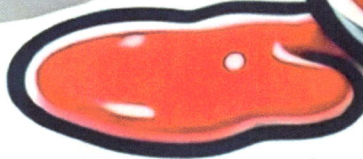

STRAWBERRY JAM

He got his hand stuck in the jar,

and now just needs a little Pam.

Have you ever heard of a pickle in a pickle?

She lost her bicycle,

bent over and found a nickel.

Or the dessert that said climbing Bully Sverlest...

is a piece of cake?

Or the lemon who bought a brand-new car

and as he pulled out of the driveway... it fell apart!

She caught on and said,
"Ooh since you like it so much,
you can wear it while you wash dishes;
the plates, bowls, spoons, and forks!"

Staring aghast at the mess on the kitchen fishscale tiles,

It dawned on him to serve a bean dip with a fishscale chip.

Cheedo's
RESTAURANT
EXIT
EXIT
Oh, how the patrons
will travel for miles!

And what happened to the two adventure-seeking peas in a pod that trod their own course in a green canoe?

Sailing alongside the salmon upstream, two peas of the same mind, chasing their one dream.

Now that these whimsical tales
have come to an end,
I hope that you have enjoyed
our little food friends.

They've gathered together up
on the stage
To send you, regardless of age,
well-wishes on your journey
through the English language.

It's your turn now, fellow
Idiomaniac, to spin some words
and phrases...

IDIOMS in this book!

You're toast!

In a jam

In a pickle

A piece of cake

Spilled the beans

The car was a lemon

Like white on rice
(also a simile)

Two peas in a pod

Trying to butter someone up

Food for thought

Food for thought...

Try using these words to create separate idioms:

Apple - nuts - vinegar – salt – plum – etc.

CHALLENGE!

Matthew needs a few animal-related idioms for a potential sequel.

Using these pieces of phrases, see if you can finish these idioms. Then say what each idiom is intended to mean (as opposed to the dictionary meaning)!

Animal Idioms!

Raining cats and _____   Meaning _____

Hold your _____   Meaning _____

A fish out _____   Meaning _____

Blind as a _____   Meaning _____

The cat's out of _____   Meaning _____

Let sleeping dogs _____   Meaning _____

A lion's _____   Meaning _____

Answers on the next page...

CHALLENGE Answers!

See how you did...

Raining cats and **dogs** = Raining very heavily

Hold your **horses** = Slow your speed - wait up!

A fish out **of water** = In unfamiliar territory

Blind as a **bat** = Cannot see very well

The cat's out of **the bag** = The secret is revealed

Let sleeping dogs **lie** = Don't upset a peaceful situation

A lion's **share** = Getting the biggest, or largest amount of something

Extra challenge!

Now go back through the whole book to see if you can spot the drawing mistakes! (Even AI is not perfect – you'll see!)

About the Author!

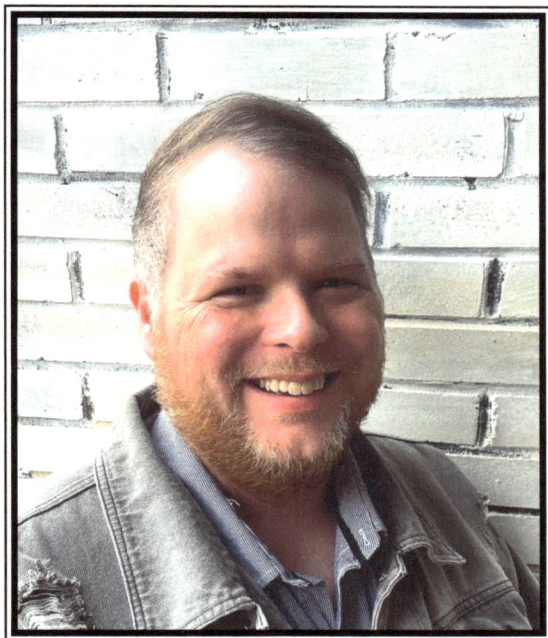

Matthew Harris

Matthew Harris is a newly published children's author from Batesville, Mississippi, where he lives with his wife, Alyssa.

A former English teacher and current coding instructor, Matthew is a life-long learner inspired by his mother's love for writing and his papaw's knack for storytelling.

Matthew's tales draw on his colorful life – he's held an octopus, narrowly avoided being a hostage, sang with a guy who sang with Elvis (every Mississippian has to have an Elvis story), danced with the unofficial Blues Brothers, and can even sing more than one note at a time! And when he's not writing or teaching, he's often strumming his guitar, cooking for friends, or sharing a story (or two) with anyone who'll listen.